THE MAKING OF

THE **X** FILES™

Fight the Future

Also published in Voyager by HarperCollins*Publishers*

The X-Files: Fight the Future
The X-Files Scrapbook

THE MAKING OF

THE **X** FILES™

Fight the Future

CREATED BY CHRIS CARTER

Adapted for Young Readers by
JODY DUNCAN

Voyager
An Imprint of HarperCollins*Publishers*

HarperCollins*Publishers*
77–85 Fulham Palace Road,
Hammersmith, London W6 8JB

A Paperback Original 1998
9 8 7 6 5 4 3 2 1

A catalogue record for this book is
available from the British Library

ISBN 0 00 648362 3

Printed and bound in Italy by Rotolito Lombarda

Cover design © 1998 by Hamagami/Carroll & Associates

Cover artwork courtesy of and
© 1998 Twentieth Century Fox Film Corporation

Designed by Laura Lindgren

CONTENTS

1

A PLAGUE AND A PROJECT (THE STORY)

The X-Files movie begins a long, long time ago, in 35,000 B.C., when much of the earth was covered in ice and snow. Two figures, primitive men, walk through the cold, windswept landscape. They are following the trail left by a mysterious creature. Three-toed tracks lead the hunters to the inside of an ice cave.

The creature is an alien—tall and thin, black-eyed and hairless, with only tiny slits for a nose and mouth. But the alien has razor-sharp teeth and long claws on his hands and feet that extend when it attacks. Suddenly the alien lashes out and fiercely attacks one of the men. One dies in the battle. The second primitive struggles and finally kills the alien. But then we see a scary black oil ooze out of the dead alien's body. It seeps into cracks on the floor and wall. The black oil seems to be alive! It creeps slowly toward the surviving primitive's chest, mouth, and eyes.

Without warning, a boy plunges through the roof of the cave. The movie has cut to the present, to Blackwood, Texas, an area outside of Dallas. A group of boys have been playing at the same cave we saw in the first scene. But now,

Stevie (Lucas Black) falls into a cave where his body is invaded by a black, oily fluid— the alien virus.

thirty-five thousand years later, the ice and snow have melted away. Instead, the cave is rocky, and in the middle of empty desert land. The boys, trying to build a fort, have dug a hole in the hard desert ground right above the cave. One of the boys—Stevie (Lucas Black)—digs too deep and suddenly falls through a hole in the earth. He falls so hard the wind is knocked out of him, but he is okay. Exploring the cave, Stevie discovers a human skull and excitedly tells his friends there are lots of bones in the cave. Suddenly, from a crack in the cave floor comes the same gooey, black substance that seeped into the floor thirty-five thousand years earlier. The black oil slowly inches toward the boy. It creeps onto his shoe, crawls under his skin, and moves through his body until even his eyes turn black and oily. Terrified by what has just happened to their friend, the boys run for help. Stevie stands frozen within the cave. The creeping alien oil has paralyzed him.

Suddenly the air is filled with sirens. Soon, there are fire trucks everywhere. Two firemen quickly climb down into the cave to rescue Stevie. Mysteriously, they don't come back. Two more firemen are sent in—and disappear, too. The bodies of all four men have been invaded and infected by the alien oil. The local fire captain is concerned when no one returns from the cave. Now the fire department has to rescue five people instead of one.

Just then, a helicopter swoops down for a landing. Dr. Ben Bronschweig (Jeffrey DeMunn) gets out. He has brought along a mysterious "hazardous materials" team. The team has seen dangerous substances like the black oil

3

The Haz-Mat team led by Dr. Ben
Bronschweig takes over the scene at the cave site.

before. They carefully and quickly carry Stevie's paralyzed
body away. The rest of his team begin setting up tents and
other equipment at the site. What the local firefighters do
not know is that Dr. Bronschweig reports to a secret orga-
nization known as "the syndicate." This cave has become
an important part of the undercover "project" the syndicate is working on. Dr. Bronschweig will set up a laboratory here to observe one of the infected firemen.

The movie action cuts to a government building one
week later. Someone has planted a bomb here. FBI agents
must hurry to find the bomb before it goes off. The FBI
has cleared out all of the people who work there, and is
now looking for where the bomb is hidden.

But two agents have decided to check the building across the street instead. One of them, Fox Mulder (David Duchovny), a handsome man with sad eyes and a quick sense of humor, has a hunch that the FBI is on the wrong track. His longtime partner, Dana Scully (Gillian

TOP/BOTTOM: Mulder and Scully speak to each other by cell phone in the federal building. Mulder is trapped in the vending machine room with the bomb. He needs Scully's help to get everyone—including him—out of the building right away.

5

Anderson), a beautiful red-haired woman, is on the roof of the building, but she speaks to him by cell phone. Together they used to be in charge of the FBI's X-Files unit. But now, that unit has been closed. In the X-Files unit they investigated, or looked into, events that were strange or difficult to explain. Now they are assigned to more common FBI duties—like checking out bomb threats.

Mulder's hunch is right. By accident, he discovers the bomb hidden in a soda machine in the building across

Mulder, Scully, and Special Agent-in-Charge Darius Michaud (Terry O'Quinn) inspect a bomb discovered within a vending machine in the federal building lobby.

the street. With Mulder locked in the vending room, Scully hurries to clear the building. She calls for help from the FBI agents next door. With just minutes to spare, Mulder is rescued by Scully and Special Agent in Charge Darius Michaud (Terry O'Quinn). Michaud orders Mulder and Scully and everyone else out of the building while he stays behind to try to defuse the bomb. As the car speeds away, the bomb goes off. The building explodes in a shower of cement, metal, and broken glass.

A bomb explodes in a Dallas building.

Mulder and Dr. Kurtzweil meet secretly to discuss government conspiracies.

The next day Mulder and Scully are at FBI head-quarters in Washington, D.C., where they are questioned by Assistant Director Jana Cassidy (Blythe Danner). She wants to know everything they saw and heard before the bombing in Dallas. The agents learn that five people were killed in the explosion. Special Agent in Charge Michaud, three firemen, and the young boy, Stevie, all died in the blast. Mulder and Scully also learn that they are being blamed for those deaths.

That night, Mulder meets Dr. Alvin Kurtzweil (Martin Landau). The doctor claims to be an old friend of Mulder's father. He also writes books about government conspiracies—plots to hide information or evidence from the public. Kurtzweil gives Mulder important news. The building in Dallas was bombed by the syndicate to hide the already dead bodies of Stevie and the three firemen. The syndicate did not want anyone to find the bodies, so they blew up the building. Kurtzweil also tells Mulder that Special Agent in Charge Michaud let the building explode because he worked for the syndicate.

Mulder is disturbed by what Kurtzweil has told him. He talks Scully into going to the naval hospital where

Scully infiltrates a hospital morgue to examine the remains of one of the bombing victims. In order to avoid discovery by the military police, she hides in the morgue freezer. When Mulder calls her on the cell phone, the ringing almost gives her away.

the bodies are being kept. At the hospital, they go straight to the cold, dark morgue—a place where dead bodies are temporarily stored. Since Scully was trained as a doctor, she carefully examines the body of one of the bombing victims. She snaps on her medical gloves and does an autopsy—or exam—on one of the firemen. Scully quickly discovers the fireman did not die from the explosion, as someone wanted the agents to believe. He died from some kind of infection. It is one she has never seen before. The victim's skin is almost

Dr. Kurtzweil meets with Mulder again to give him more information.

see-through and feels like sticky gelatin. His internal organs—like his heart, liver, and kidneys—have been partially eaten away by the virus.

While Scully examines the body, Mulder meets with Kurtzweil again. The doctor warns Mulder that the syndicate is involved in a secret government "project" to deliberately release a terrible plague. He says the syndicate has been working on the project for over fifty years! But Kurtzweil can't or won't give Mulder any proof—he tells him to go to Dallas to search for the truth.

With this new information, Mulder asks Scully to meet him at the FBI field office in Dallas, Texas. There they look at the scattered waste from the bombed building. The two agents are shown ancient pieces of bone called fossils which were found at the bomb site. The FBI field agent tells them the fossils had originally been found at an archaeological dig site and had been kept in an office in the building that exploded. Scully looks at the bone fossils under a microscope. The same virus that killed the fireman is also in the fossils.

Back at the cave site, the Cigarette-Smoking Man (William B. Davis) arrives in a black helicopter to talk to Dr. Bronschweig. Dr. Bronschweig's team has set up a high-tech lab at the site, and it is very cold inside. The doctor explains that they have lowered the temperature to freezing to slow the development of the virus. They view the body of one of the firemen, who is barely still alive. His skin is gray and gelatinous, like the bodies Scully saw at the hospital, and there seems to be something *alive* inside him. Something that *blinks*. The virus has mutated into a living organism!

Dr. Bronschweig asks the Cigarette-Smoking Man if they should destroy the body before the new organism grows any larger. "No," answers the Cigarette-Smoking Man, "we need to try our vaccine on it."

After the Cigarette-Smoking Man leaves, Dr. Bronschweig returns to the cave to administer the vaccine, only to find the infected fireman's chest ripped wide open. The organism that was growing inside of him is gone. Seconds later, the fully grown alien savagely attacks the doctor with his sharp claws. Dr. Bronschweig

Dr. Bronschweig attempts to escape from the alien.

calls for help, but the crew, worried that he is now infected, quickly fills the cave hole with dirt so the creature cannot get away. They bury Bronschweig and the alien forever.

When Mulder and Scully go to the cave site to investigate, all they see is a brand-new playground. They question Stevie's playmates, and learn that tanker trucks left the playground just minutes earlier. The two agents speed away to see if they can find the trucks. They drive for

Despite having their silence bought with new bikes,
Stevie's playmates reluctantly inform Mulder and Scully
that mysterious tanker trucks left the site just minutes earlier.

ABOVE: Mulder and Scully inspect the bee dome interior.

RIGHT: Mulder and Scully spot the approaching helicopters.

hours without seeing anything until they finally reach a dead end at a railroad crossing. Just when Mulder and Scully are about to give up, a train comes by carrying the tanker trucks.

The agents follow the train until it stops at a corn-field. Mulder and Scully are confused about what a corn-field would be doing in the middle of the desert. There are several strange, giant, white domes in the middle of the cornfield. They enter one of the white domes, but are suddenly chased out by swarms of bees. When they get outside, mysterious, low-flying helicopters chase them through the cornfield.

Mulder and Scully make it back to Washington, D.C. Although Scully does not know it, one of the bees is hiding in her jacket. Scully tells Assistant Director Cassidy that she and Mulder went back to Dallas and discovered evidence that the bombing was a cover-up.

Later Scully goes to Mulder's apartment to tell him she is going to quit the FBI because she has been assigned to another city. Mulder and Scully have worked together for a long time and have developed a close friendship and deep respect for each other. Mulder asks

Scully goes to Mulder's apartment to tell him she plans to leave the FBI.

Mulder wakes up in the hospital after being shot. Assistant Director
Skinner (Mitch Pileggi) and the Lone Gunman are there.

her not to quit. He doesn't know if he can continue on
without her.

Just then, the bee hiding in Scully's jacket stings her
and she falls to the floor in Mulder's hallway. Mulder calls
an ambulance and a uniformed medical team comes to
take Scully away. But they are not real ambulance drivers. When Mulder asks which hospital they will be taking Scully to, the driver shoots Mulder. He is wounded in
the head. As the ambulance pulls away the real ambulance pulls up and sees Mulder lying on the ground.

Later, Scully's unconscious body is put into a cryolit-
ter—a kind of clear refrigerated box. It is loaded onto a
plane at the airport, headed for the Antarctic.

Mulder wakes up in a Washington hospital. Luckily, he is not badly hurt. His friends the Lone Gunmen (Bruce Harwood, Dean Haglund, and Tom Braidwood) are there. The Lone Gunmen have helped Mulder in the past. They tell Mulder someone listened to his phone call and sent a fake ambulance. Mulder asks the Lone Gunmen to help him escape from the hospital. He knows he has got to find Scully. He arranges to meet Kurtzweil, hoping the doctor can tell him where Scully is.

When Mulder arrives at the meeting place, he doesn't find Kurtzweil. Instead Mulder runs into the Well-Manicured Man (John Neville), who is involved with the syndicate. He gives Mulder Scully's location, as well as the vaccine that can save her life, but only if it is given to her in the next ninety-six hours. He also tells Mulder that the virus *is* extraterrestrial. The shadowy syndicate has been working with the aliens. But the syndicate has also been secretly developing the vaccine to protect the members and their families from the virus. Mulder doesn't know if he should trust the Well-Manicured Man. He thinks the Well-Manicured Man has killed Kurtzweil and put his body in the trunk of his car!

The Well-Manicured Man drops Mulder off and tells him to go find Scully because only her science can save them. As soon as the Well-Manicured Man gets back in his car, it bursts into flames. The Well-Manicured Man is dead and Mulder runs off, realizing that time is running out.

Mulder looks on as the Well-Manicured Man's car explodes.

Next, the movie cuts to a snow tractor in Antarctica. We see Mulder, searching for Scully over the cold, grim land. He finds an ice station and, through binoculars, sees the Cigarette-Smoking Man leaving. As Mulder gets close to the station on foot, he suddenly plunges through the ice and tumbles down a deep ice shaft. He lands on what seems like a hard metal object covered with snow and ice. He lowers himself through a steam vent and crawls through the cramped passageway. It finally widens to become a huge and strange indoor space. Mulder doesn't know it yet, but he has stumbled into an alien spaceship, hidden beneath the ice.

Climbing down to the hallways below, Mulder spots Scully in one of the thousands of cryopods—iced units in which bodies infected by the virus are kept. These bodies—called "hosts" because they host the virus so it can grow—are in a frozen state, but alive. Mulder breaks through the icy covering of the pod. He shoots the vaccine into Scully's shoulder with a needle. In moments, Scully begins to awaken. The tube in her mouth shrivels up and Mulder pulls it out so she can breathe.

Suddenly the whole ship shudders and rumbles. The vaccine has woken up the ship, too. The inside of the ship begins to warm up. The heat makes the icy cryopod coverings melt. The aliens begin to wriggle around inside the host bodies. Mulder carries Scully back to the top of the ship. Scully stops breathing. While Mulder gives her CPR, the aliens begin to hatch from the bodies and

After discovering Scully within one of the spaceship
cryopods, Mulder breaks through the thick icy covering
and injects her with the life-saving antidote.

break free of the cryopods. Scully regains consciousness just in time to escape the aliens.

With one of the creatures not far behind, Mulder gets Scully to the top of the ship. They are out just in time, but the whole ice field is shaking and collapsing beneath their feet. Under the ice, the ship begins to rise. Mulder and Scully run for their lives, just a few feet ahead of the collapsing ice. Suddenly, they fall into a hole. Moments later, they land on what appears to be a section of the rising spaceship! The agents fall off the ship and land on the icy ground. Scully lies unconscious as Mulder watches the eerie ship rise higher and higher, until it is surrounded by swirling clouds and disappears into the sky.

After Mulder and Scully's escape from the ship, the ice field collapses around them.

Back in Washington, Scully meets with Assistant Director Cassidy and other FBI officials. They question her about her report, in which she tells the story of what happened to her and Mulder. Assistant Director Cassidy thinks the report is too unbelievable to be true. Besides, there is no evidence to prove anything in Scully's report.

Scully hands Cassidy a vial containing a dead bumblebee, the only evidence left.

Later we see Mulder reading the newspaper. He sees a story about a virus outbreak in Texas, and he knows it is a cover-up. Scully comes over and he shows her the story. Mulder is frustrated and angry, but Scully is more hopeful. She has told the officials everything that happened. Mulder tells her that she should give up his hopeless cause, but she says if they quit now the bad guys will have won.

The last scene takes place in Tunisia. We see a man walking along rows and rows of corn. It is the Cigarette-Smoking Man. He has come to talk with Conrad Strughold (Armin Mueller-Stahl), another member of the syndicate. The Cigarette-Smoking Man tells Strughold that Mulder is still on the case. Strughold tells him not to worry. One man alone cannot fight the future. "Yesterday," says the Cigarette-Smoking Man, "I received this." He hands Strughold a telegram which reads:

X-Files re-opened. Stop. Please advise. Stop.

Strughold sighs and drops the telegram, and walks back into the massive cornfield.

2

SCRIPTS, SCOUTS, AND STORYBOARDS

(PREPARING THE MOVIE)

Working out the story for *The X-Files* was just the first step in making the movie. There were many other things that had to be done before filming could even begin. One of the first and most important tasks was writing the script, or screenplay. The screenplay is about 120 pages long. It describes all of the action that will happen. It has all of the actors' lines written down. It also says what the camera should do and what each shot should look like on the movie screen—a close-up on an actor, for example, or a wide shot that will show a very large area.

The pages in the screenplay for the opening scene with the primitive men read like this:

Chris Carter on location in California City.

Fade in:

1 Ext. (exterior) Snowscape

A blinding white screen, under which we hear an ominous rumble. As the rumble builds, two black figures appear on what now has resolved into a distant horizon. From their movements, we can see that the figures are men, moving along a windswept ice sheet in an otherwise featureless land.

A legend appears: North Texas, 35,000 B.C.

Closer on the two men. Continuing toward us, we can now see that they are dressed in crude garments made of animal skins. If we squint, we can see that their hair is long, their jutting foreheads significant of primitive Homo sapiens. They continue toward us, the wind beating against them. Camera is craning down to the snow that lies before them. To large three-toed tracks.

Frank Spotnitz, Rob Bowman, Dan Sackheim, and Chris Carter on stage at Fox.

The *X-Files* movie story was written by Chris Carter and Frank Spotnitz. Carter then used the story to write the screenplay. Chris Carter is the creator and executive producer of *The X-Files* television show. Frank Spotnitz is the co-executive producer. A producer is in charge of the television show or movie being made. He or she is the boss.

Once the screenplay was written, Carter hired Rob Bowman to direct the movie. He also hired Daniel Sackheim and Lata Ryan to help him produce it. Together, the producers and the director hired the actors who would play the leading roles in the movie. You may already know many of these actors. They have been playing important roles on *The X-Files* television show for several years. These actors include David Duchovny as Agent Fox Mulder and Gillian Anderson as Agent Dana Scully. Mitch Pileggi plays the role of Assistant Director Walter Skinner, William B. Davis is the Cigarette-Smoking Man, and John Neville plays the Well-Manicured Man.

The new roles written just for the movie also had to be filled by actors —or cast. Dr. Alvin Kurtzweil, the author who helps Mulder and Scully to find the true nature of the project, is played by Martin

Well-known actor Martin Landau plays Dr. Kurtzweil.

Landau. He is a well-known actor who won an Academy Award for his role as Bela Lugosi in *Ed Wood* in 1994. Other famous actors were hired for the movie, too. Blythe Danner plays Assistant Director Jana Cassidy, Armin Mueller-Stahl plays the role of syndicate elder Conrad Strugold, and Glenne Headly plays a barmaid.

By the time the movie was finished, more than five hundred people had worked on it! These were not just actors. Lighting, camera, special effects, and visual effects crews all put in hours of work. Extras—actors who do not have speaking roles—and wardrobe and makeup crews were also on the set every day. Try counting all the names that roll by at the end of a movie. You'll see just how many people it takes "behind the scenes" to bring a movie to the big screen.

When all the actors and crews had been hired, the director and producers began going on location scouts. A location scout is when filmmakers travel to many places to look for just the right place to film their movie. Some of the scenes in the screenplay, for example, called for a desert area outside Dallas, Texas. The filmmakers scouted many desert areas in Texas and in California. They had to find the right spot for the scene where Stevie falls into the cave, and for the scene where Mulder and Scully discover a mysterious cornfield.

It costs a lot of money to take film equipment and cast and crew members long distances. So the moviemakers looked for places that weren't too far away from their home base at Twentieth Century Fox studio in

"Scully, listen to me."

"You've got about fourteen minutes to get this building evacuated."

"We're under pressure to give an accurate picture of what happened in the Dallas explosion to the Attorney General."

"If they want someone to blame, they can blame me. Agent Scully doesn't deserve this."

"I think that just about does it, Spooky."

"It's left the body. I think it's gestated—"

"Help! I nee

've been forced to reassess our role in Colonization."

"This is weird, Mulder. Any thoughts on why anybody would be growing corn in the middle of the desert?"

"Not unless those are giant Jiffy Pop poppers out there."

"You found something?"
"Yes. On the Texas border. Some kind of experiment."

"Find Agent Scully."

"Only then will you realize the scope and grandeur of the Project."

"Breathe!"

"Can you *breathe?*"

"Come on . . . it's time to go."

"One man alone cannot fight the future."

Los Angeles. Many shots of Dallas or Washington, D.C, for example, were actually filmed in downtown Los Angeles. Filmmakers kept palm and citrus trees and telltale street signs carefully from the view of the camera. To moviegoers, the scene looks like it was filmed in Dallas or Washington, D.C.

While the producers were doing the location scouts, director Rob Bowman was spending every day with artists Gabriel Hardman and Roy Bihun. Together, they were storyboarding the movie. Storyboards are almost like comic books—done in black and white—that show every single shot of the movie. For example, the scene in which Dr. Bronschweig is attacked by the alien might be shown—or illustrated—in drawings of the doctor facing toward the camera, with the alien hiding behind him.

Storyboard artist Gabriel Hardman works as spaceship interior dummies look on.

On location, Rob Bowman goes over the storyboards for the day's filming.

Next, there might be a drawing of Dr. Bronschweig turning around and seeing the alien, his eyes opened wide in fright. After that might be a drawing of the alien's claw reaching toward Dr. Bronschweig's face.

Every moment of every scene was worked out and sketched in storyboard form. This was done so that Rob Bowman would know where to put his cameras and how to direct the actors once he got on the set. "Storyboarding is really the process of creating the movie," Bowman explained. "When it was done, I had a storyboard book that was thicker than *Webster's Unabridged Dictionary.*" On the set, the storyboards were always posted on a big board. The board sat next to Bowman's director's chair. He could study them while he was shooting the movie.

In addition to storyboarding, finding locations, casting, and hiring the movie crew, many other jobs had to be done in the few weeks before the movie shoot. Sets had to be designed. Wardrobe for all of the actors and extras had to be found. Lights had to be set up on stages and equipment had to be rented. It was a whirlwind of activity for all of the moviemakers. With only ten weeks to finish all these jobs, they barely had enough time to prepare the movie. The director and producers and other crew members worked seven days a week throughout that period to get everything done in time. And they did. On June 9, 1997, cameras rolled on *The X-Files* feature film, as scheduled.

3

MONSTERS AND MAKEUPS

(MAKEUP EFFECTS)

A company called Amalgamated Dynamics Incorporated (ADI) created most of the creature and makeup effects for *The X-Files* movie. The makeup effects artists at ADI have been involved in some of the biggest movies of the past few years. They created the lion, alligator, and other animals for *Jumanji*. They also made the giant bugs you might have seen in *Starship Troopers* and aliens for the last two *Alien* movies.

The first thing ADI did for *The X-Files* was to create makeups to turn actors Craig Davis and Carrick O'Quinn into the primitive men seen at the beginning of the movie. To design the makeups, the artists took a "life-cast" of each actor. They did this by covering his whole head with a kind of plaster. Then they let the plaster dry and very carefully removed the front and back halves. Both plaster halves could then be filled with clay or some other material.

The makeup that turned one of the actors into
a primitive man took more than three hours to apply.

After the plaster lifecasts were filled, the material hardened. The plaster shell was removed. What was left gave the makeup artists perfect sculptures of the actors' heads. These sculptures were used by the artists to create the look of the primitive men. They did this by adding more sculpted pieces to the plaster heads. Clay was added to the sides of the nose, for example, to make it look wider. More clay pieces were added to make the jaw look longer and to make the forehead stick out like a primitive man's. The new sculptures now looked like primitives because of the added pieces. The artists then took another casting from the new sculptures, making foam rubber pieces that could be glued onto the actors' faces.

Since the makeups had been designed on the sculptured heads of the actors, they fit each actor's face exactly.

Each makeup was made of three foam latex pieces. One piece covered the top of the actor's head and his ears. A second piece covered the eyebrows, nose, cheeks, and upper lip. A third piece fit over the chin and lower lip. The foam rubber pieces—called "appliances"—were glued onto the actor's head and face. Then they were blended with his real skin with thick "pancake" makeup. The actors also wore dark brown contact lenses and false teeth that were yellow and crooked. On location, the makeups were applied by makeup artist Lance Anderson and his makeup team. At first, it took more than three hours to apply each makeup. With practice, the team got the time down to just over two hours.

One of the stars of *The X-Files* feature film is the alien. He is a tall, thin creature with large black eyes and claws on his hands and feet. The creature was also designed by ADI. Artists at the studio first did sketches of the alien to show to Chris Carter and Rob Bowman and the producers. The producers and director chose the alien sketch they liked best. ADI sculptors then created ten-inch-tall "maquettes"—little statues of the alien that showed everyone what he would look like in three dimensions. The maquettes were also painted so Carter and Bowman could see how the alien's skin would appear and what color it would be.

When Carter and Bowman gave the go-ahead, ADI built two mechanical heads for the alien. One was called

Alec Gillis and Tom Woodruff present
a maquette of the creature for approval.

a "hero head" because it was used for close-ups of the
creature. It was operated by radio control joysticks, much
like the controllers that are used on remote-control cars.
These controllers could make the creature's eyes blink, its
eyebrows raise and lower, and its lips snarl. A second,
stunt head was used for shots of the alien opening its
mouth wide as it attacked its victims. The opening of the
jaw was the stunt head's only movement. It was much
simpler to work than the hero head. The jaw was opened

with cables that came out of the back, to a controller held by a puppeteer.

Only one of the heads was worn at a time. The head was worn by Tom Woodruff. He is a makeup effects artist who also performs as creatures and monsters for movies. For example, he was the squid-type monster in *Leviathan*, and an alien in *Alien Resurrection*. Woodruff plays these roles wearing specially made suits. For *The X-Files*, he wore a foam rubber suit and the mechanical head.

To make the suits and heads, the artists from ADI first made a life-sized sculpture of the alien over a casting of Woodruff's body. They had to be sure the finished suit would fit on the creature performer. Molds were then taken by pressing a special material against the sculpture. The material hardened, and was then pulled away. This left indents—called impressions—of the alien's head and body in the mold. These impressions were much like what you would get if you pressed a large flat sheet of dough onto your face. When you pulled it away, you would have the impression of your face in the dough.

Those molds were then filled with liquid foam rubber and put into ovens to bake. The baking process was done when the rubber had hardened. The artists then carefully peeled the rubber "skin" out of the molds. Those skins were attached to a metal skull for the heads. The skins for the body were attached to a special Lycra suit. It looked very much like a wet suit a scuba diver would wear. Hands and feet were also made with rubber skin and long, sharp claws. Several alien suits and heads were made, just in case one of them was damaged during filming.

When the director was ready to shoot a scene with the alien, Tom Woodruff would get into the skintight bodysuit first. He would then put the mechanical head on over his own head. Since the eyes in the head were like dark marbles, and the nose and mouth were only tiny slits, Woodruff could not see out of the head. He had to perform all of his scenes blind!

Just before the director called "Action!", members of the ADI team sprayed the marble eyes with mist. This made them look watery and alive. The skin of the head and body would also be covered with wet, shiny slime to make it look alive.

ADI artists at work on the alien embryo.

The ADI shop, populated by host dummies.

In some scenes, we see the aliens curled up inside clear host bodies. For those scenes, copies of the alien suit that Tom Woodruff wore were cut down. They were made smaller, then tucked and curled up to fit inside fake human bodies, or dummies. Alien heads were also placed inside the dummy bodies. These heads were operated from behind by puppeteers. Each fake body was open in the back. The puppeteer could hide behind the dummy, reach his hands in and move the alien around to make it look as if it were alive and wiggling inside the body. Movement of the alien's face was radio-controlled.

An ADI makeup effects artist punches
hair into the scalp of one of the host bodies.

ADI also made two mechanical human host bodies. These were used for the scene in the spaceship in which the aliens begin to "hatch" from their hosts. The bodies had an inner core made of hard plastic. It was sculpted and painted to look like bones and organs that are inside human bodies. That core was covered with silicone. Silicone is a clear material that looks and feels like the see-through, gelatinlike flesh of the infected bodies. The aliens were then placed inside their new human host bodies. They could be seen through the clear silicone skin. The fake bodies—complete with aliens inside—were then placed inside cryopods on the

OPPOSITE: One of the cryopods aboard the
alien ship where the host bodies were kept.

spaceship set. They were operated from off-camera by puppeteers on mechanical controllers. The puppeteers made the bodies move and squirm as the aliens broke free.

Other cryopods are lined up in the background and were filled with non-moving dummies. These were built by KNB Effects Group, a company that had made makeup effects for *The X-Files* television show on many

A KNB Effects artist sculpts a host body.

occasions. These fourteen bodies—seven males and seven females—were also made with silicone skins and plastic cores. At first, KNB placed small foam rubber aliens inside the swollen bellies of some of the dummies. But the aliens did not show up clearly enough through the silicone skins. The makeup artists took out the foam puppets, and simply painted the alien right onto the core.

One of the bodies seen in a spaceship cryopod is FBI Agent Scully. Since she has only recently been infected by the alien virus, her skin is not yet see-through. She looks as if she is only sleeping inside the cryopod. Because Gillian Anderson could not be closed up inside the cryopod, KNB had to make up a dummy for her body. This meant that Gillian Anderson had to have a lifecast done. The plaster material was spread all over her face, covering her eyes, mouth, nose, and ears. Two straws were put into her nostrils to keep her air passages clear. They made it possible for her to breathe while the plaster hardened on her face and head.

Another host body, a fireman, is seen being studied inside the cave laboratory run by Dr. Bronschweig. That body, like the others, had to appear see-through. Visible inside the fireman's clear skin is an alien embryo—a tiny version of the creature. ADI created a movable embryo and placed it inside a movable fireman body. The actor playing the fireman was cast from head to toe. From that casting, the makeup artists made a copy of the actor. Then they sculpted the copy, giving it shrunken arms and legs. It also had a swollen belly, where the embryo would

Both shots of Gillian Anderson and a Scully dummy built by KNB
were used to create this scene. But the face we actually
see here is the real Gillian Anderson.

be growing. Molds were then taken from the new sculpture and filled with silicone to make the fireman's body. Veins—which carry blood throughout the body—and other body parts were painted onto a hard plastic core that was placed inside the clear body. More veins were painted on the silicone skin. Fake eyes and teeth, made of hard plastics—called acrylics—were fitted into the head. Also, to make the body

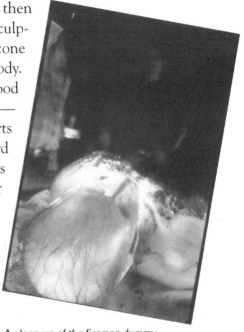

A close-up of the fireman dummy.

look absolutely real, human hairs were punched into the silicone skin, one strand of hair at a time.

The ADI puppeteers used cable and radio controls to make the fireman's eyes open and close, his head roll, and his jaw open. They could even make his chest move in and out as if he were breathing, and his heart—seen through his clear skin—beat.

The embryo alien inside the body was made from foam rubber. It had a movable, mechanical head that worked using radio-control joysticks. The radio control made the embryo blink and his jaw open and close. To make his body move, rods were attached to the puppet in the back. Puppeteers could hide behind the fireman body and pull on these rods, making the alien embryo wiggle and shift inside the fireman's body. "It was a really wonderful effect," said Tom Woodruff. "The fireman was rolling his head, and breathing in and out. And inside, you could see this little alien blinking. When we brought this puppet to the set and first operated it, everyone gasped. They were amazed."

Later in the movie, the alien embryo grows to full size. It hatches from the fireman, leaving only his dead,

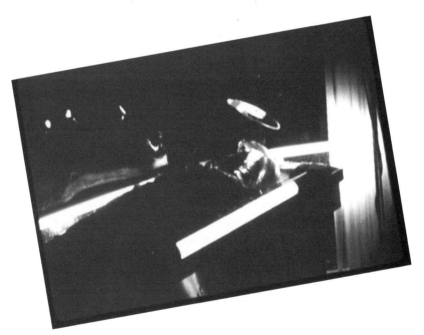

The cave fireman was actually a moveable puppet built by ADI.

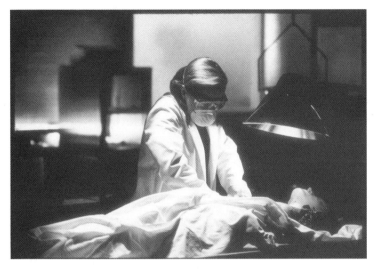

Scully performs a secret autopsy on the dead fireman,
whose body was infected by the alien virus.

shrunken body. For that effect, ADI made a second version of the fireman that had more shrunken-looking arms
and legs. It also had a belly area that was sculpted and
painted to look as if it had been ripped open by the alien.

Another fireman body was needed for the scene at
the hospital morgue. Scully sneaks in to examine the
dead body, but the virus has eaten away at his blood and
internal organs. It has left only a pale, almost see-through
body. The morgue fireman was another makeup effect,
created by KNB Effects Group. A lifecast was taken of
the actor who was playing the fireman in the movie. Silicone was poured into the molds to make the body. Inside
the clear silicone skin was a hard plastic skeleton that

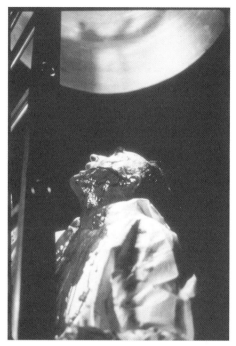

ADI designed the make-up for a bloody
Dr. Bronschweig.

was painted to look like bones and muscles.

The final makeup effect created for *The X-Files* movie was one for the scene in which Bronschweig is attacked by an alien. The actor playing Bronschweig, Jeffrey De-Munn, had to be made up to look like his face had been attacked by the creature's sharp claws. A lifecast was taken of the actor, and the attack makeup was designed over that casting. Several foam rubber makeup pieces were glued onto the actor's face. Hidden underneath the pieces were tubes that ran out the back of his head to a pump system. Fake blood was pumped through the tubes, to make Bronschweig look as if he was bleeding after the alien attack.

4

ICE CAPS, CAVES, AND CORNFIELDS

(LOCATIONS AND SETS)

The X-Files movie was filmed either on sets built at Twentieth Century Fox studio, or "on location." That is when the cast and crew and equipment are moved to a place outside the studio for filming. Sometimes those places were far away. Sometimes they were nearby.

Most of the location scenes in *The X-Files* were filmed in areas near to Los Angeles. Some long-distance locations were needed, though. The production moved to a glacier north of Vancouver, British Columbia, in Canada for scenes showing Mulder looking for Scully in Antarctica. The glacier, called the Pemberton Ice Cap, was also used for the first scene in the movie, where two primitive men follow alien tracks in the snow.

Before the actors, director, and crew went to the glacier, members of the production's art department flew there to build the ice station set. The glacier was very far away from any town or people. Crew members and set

Filming began on a glacier two hours north of Vancouver, British Columbia.

David Duchovny, William B. Davis, and co-producer
Frank Spotnitz at the glacier location.

48

pieces actually had to be flown into the site every day by helicopter! Set pieces, lights, and camera equipment were loaded into containers that hung from the bottom of the helicopters. As the helicopters flew over the filming spot, they released the containers, dropping them to the ground.

Sometimes, the helicopters could not get into the glacier because of bad weather or thick clouds. At those times, the movie crews would have to wait at their hotel until the weather cleared. Then they could get to the site for filming. Once, crew members even had to spend a night on the glacier because the helicopters could not get in to pick them up! The crew slept inside the ice station set to keep warm, with only health fruit bars to eat. Fortunately, the set builders were used to harsh weather. They lived near the glacier all year around. "It was actually a great adventure," recalled art director Marc Fisichella, one of the crew members stranded on the ice cap. "Not too many people get to spend the night on a glacier!"

In the opening scene of the movie, the two primitives enter an ice cave, hunting a mysterious creature. The ice cap had real ice caves, but the crew could not get shots of them in June. The caves were completely covered with ice and snow then. The warm summer months melted the snow enough to open the ice caves. When the crew returned to the glacier in September they were able to shoot that part of the scene.

Most of the movie was shot much closer to Los Angeles. One movie location was in California City, a town in

David Duchovny and producer Chris Carter talk on location in California City.

the Mojave Desert. It is about an hour-and-a-half's drive from Los Angeles. The California City location was used for the scene where Stevie falls into a cave and his friends run for help. The same location was used for the later scene in which Mulder and Scully arrive to look at the cave, but find only a playground. Both scenes were supposed to take place near Dallas, Texas. But since the desert in California City looked very much like the Texas desert the producers decided to go there instead.

Imagine being outdoors all day, in the middle of a desert in July! That is what the actors and crew for *The X-Files* had to do for three days. The temperatures in the middle of the day reached 115 degrees. Crew members

The young actors, with director Rob Bowman, watch
the scene they just shot on a monitor.

had to drink a lot of water to keep their bodies healthy
and cool. They also had to put on plenty of sunscreen so
they wouldn't burn.

A fourteen-foot hole was dug at the location in California City. It was used for scenes showing Stevie's friends
around the opening to the cave, and firemen climbing
into the opening to rescue the young boy. The inside of
the cave was actually built as a set at the studio. But the
hole at the desert location had to be deep enough to
make it look as if the firemen were entering the cave.

After the scorching sun and heat of California City,
the movie crew was happy to move to night shooting in
Bakersfield, California. Normally, the night shoots went

Although all of the cave interiors would be shot on a
set built on stage at Fox, the exterior cave opening
was simulated at the location by a 14-foot-deep hole.

from about six o'clock in the evening to six o'clock in
the morning. The cast and crew would then sleep during
the day.

In Bakersfield, the production filmed scenes in a real
eight-acre cornfield. One of the problems for the movie
crew was lighting the huge cornfield brightly enough that
it would show up on film. You may have had experience
in trying to take a picture in the dark. When the picture

is developed, all you get is a black square. The same thing happens with movie cameras—if there isn't enough light, nothing shows up! To light the entire eight acres of the cornfield, the movie crew had to set up huge movie lights on towers and cranes all around the area.

In the middle of the cornfield were two giant bee domes, 30 feet tall and 140 feet long. They were made of the same kind of material that is used to make parachutes. The director and the producers wanted the bee domes to glow like giant lanterns in the cornfield. So the domes were filled with huge movie lights on the inside.

In the movie, Mulder and Scully are chased through the cornfield by mysterious helicopters. The dark gray

The agents' pursuit of the tankers leads them to a
giant cornfield, inhabited by strange, glowing bee domes.

53

helicopters were very difficult to see in the night sky. To make them easier to see, white stripes were painted on their rotor blades. Searchlights on the helicopters also helped to light up the cornfield below.

The production company for *The X-Files* went to other locations, too. Many were in Los Angeles, such as the abandoned sixteen-story building that was used for the federal building that explodes. Real Los Angeles alleyways were filmed for Mulder's secret Washington meetings with Kurtzweil, the author who has information

The dangerous low-flying helicopter
stunts were coordinated by David Paris.

John Neville as the Well-Manacured Man, Armin Mueller-Stahl as Conrad Strughold, and William B. Davis as the Cigarette-Smoking Man, on the Pasadena set of the London office where the syndicate meets.

about the alien "project." Real apartment buildings were used to show the outsides of Kurtzweil's and Mulder's apartments. The inside of Mulder's apartment was not in a real building. The rooms were built and filmed on stage. A real mansion in nearby Pasadena was used for the Well-Manicured Man's estate. A dining club at a college in Pasadena, Cal Tech, served as the rooms in the men's club where the syndicate elders meet to discuss the project. Shots of Scully's frozen body being boarded onto a plane were filmed at Los Angeles International Airport.

The most long-distance location was London, England. A small crew of about forty people went there to shoot the outside of the men's club. Southern California had done a good job of standing in for Washington and Texas. But Los Angeles had no red double-decker buses, no Big Ben, no cars with the drivers on the right side, and no River Thames. Even movie magic couldn't make Los Angeles look like London!

When the movie company wasn't on location, it was filming on sets at Twentieth Century Fox. These sets were first designed in paintings and sketches. These were done by Chris Nowak, the production designer, and Tim Flattery and Jim Martin, the concept illustrators. After Chris Carter and the other filmmakers had approved these paintings and drawings, blueprints were made. Blueprints are also a kind of drawing, but they show the exact measurements of every wall and every door and every structure. With those blueprints, construction coordinator Bill Iiams and his crew could build the sets exactly as they were drawn.

The sets were built on soundstages—huge, empty spaces that are about the same size as airplane hangars. One of the most important sets built at the studio was the spaceship interior that Mulder discovers after falling through the ice in Antarctica. After climbing down into an air tunnel, Mulder comes upon a balcony, overlooking the huge interior of the ship. The production's art department and construction crews worked together to build a set that filled the whole soundstage. The set was made up of gigantic tubes and long hallways. These were filled with cryopods, the ice-covered units that keep alien-

A shot of the interior hallway aboard the space craft.

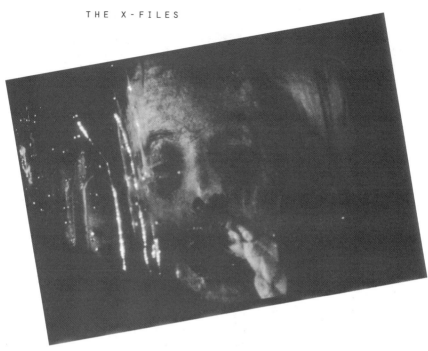

A close-up of a host body inside a cryopod.

infected host bodies alive, but in a frozen, sleeping state. The special effects crew built the cryopods out of acrylics and fiberglass. Materials made to break easily covered the front of the cryopods. The clear material looked just like ice. It also allowed the puppeteers who were moving the aliens to break the creature through the "ice" fairly easily during the hatching scene.

Another important set built at the studio was a field of ice. It was used for the shots of Mulder and Scully running as the spaceship rises from the ice and lifts off into the sky. Both fake snow and real chipped ice were spread

The film crew sets up on the interior hallway set.

David Duchovny awaits a shot setup on the
exterior spaceship set, built on Stage 15 at Fox.

out over a platform that was twenty-five feet wide and ninety feet long. The platform was raised eight feet off the stage floor. The space under the platform made room for steam generators that were used to create exploding geysers—or fountains—of ice on the set. Mulder and Scully were seen running through these geysers. The geysers made it look as if the entire ice field was caving in as the spaceship below began to rise. The platform also allowed the crew to rig a system to drain the melted ice, which formed a pool of water below.

To keep the ice on the set from melting too quickly, the temperature was lowered to about forty degrees. Huge air conditioners blew on the set all day. Keeping the stage cold enough was especially difficult. The daytime scene

Mulder and Scully climb up through a hole in the ice to momentary safety.

Duchovny and Anderson jump into a hole formed as the ice crumbles around the rising spaceship. A green screen was placed at the end of the set to allow use of special effects.

required many bright—and very hot—lights. All day long, while shooting on the ice field set, crew members were going from the hot ninety-degree weather outside, into the winter-like forty-degree weather inside the stage.

The last big stage set built for the movie was the cave. The cave set actually had to look like three different caves in the movie. First, it is the ice cave that the primitive men track the alien through at the beginning of the movie. Then it is the rocky, dry cave that Stevie falls into. Later, the same cave looks very different after Dr. Bronschweig has put in all of his high-tech testing and monitoring equipment.

The crew prepares to shoot Bronschweig after his attack by the alien.

Dr. Bronschweig's high-tech equipment inside the cave set.

To build the cave set, wooden frames were covered with plaster that was then sculpted into the cave formations. The stalagmites—formations that grow up from the floor of a cave—and stalactites—formations that grow down from the ceiling—were painted in earthy, rock-like colors.

For the filming of the ice cave, separately built "ice walls"—made of clear acrylics and fiberglass to look like ice—were wheeled into place. The entire set was then covered with chipped ice and fake snow. It was so cold that everyone could see their breath frozen in the air. When it was time to shoot the desert cave scenes, all of that ice and snow was cleaned out of the stage. It was shoveled into wheelbarrows and dumped outside. Finally, the ice walls were removed.

Monitors, computers, and a "containment unit" were all brought in and set up on the cave for the scenes with Dr. Bronschweig and his team. A "containment unit" is a tent that works much like the cryopods in the spaceship, in which the infected fireman is kept alive. The fireman seen inside the containment tent was a puppet built by ADI, operated from off-camera.

5

BOMBS, BURNS, AND BEES

(SPECIAL EFFECTS)

Special effects coordinator Paul Lombardi and Hollywood Special Effects—a company that does special effects for movies—gave *The X-Files* movie some of its most exciting moments.

One of those unforgettable moments happens near the beginning of the movie. Mulder and Scully find a bomb in the snack room of a government building in Dallas, Texas. As the bomb ticks down, other FBI agents clear everyone out of the building. Mulder and Scully run out at the last minute. Just as the agents jump into their waiting car, the bomb goes off, and the building is destroyed in a huge explosion.

The production company found an empty sixteen-story building where they could set off the explosion. It was called the UNOCAL building, and it was located in downtown Los Angeles. Preparing to film the explosion took many weeks. First, they had to get permission from

Director Rob Bowman (with arm raised) discusses a rooftop shot
with executive producer Lata Ryan, director of photography
Ward Russell, and other key members of the crew.

the Los Angeles Fire Department. Firemen and fire trucks
would be there when the explosion went off. They would
make sure everything was safe and put out fires, just in
case something went wrong.

Next, the film crew built a "facade" in front of the
UNOCAL building. A facade is a fake front of a building. It was made of glass and aluminum, and was built to
look as if it were a part of the real building. The facade
went from the street level, up through the second story of
the building. "The facade matched the architecture of
the building," explained production designer Chris
Nowak. "So when you looked at it from the front, it

didn't look as if anything had been done to the building at all. The facade blended into the building perfectly."

To make sure that the real building would not burn when the facade was blown up, the crew also put up "fire walls." Fire walls are made of sheetrock which will not burn. The walls were placed between the facade and the real structure.

Once the facade was built, a crew from Hollywood Special Effects went in. Their job was to attach primer cord, an explosive, to key sections of the false front. The effects crew also put in drums of propane gas. These could be sparked to form large balls of fire at the push of a button.

The explosion was set off on a Saturday evening in June 1997—a whole year before the movie would open

Special effects artists set off an explosion.

Paul Lombardi's special effects crew were responsible for all explosions.

in theaters! Fourteen movie cameras were set up around the building. This was done to make sure that all the action would be captured on film. The explosion could be filmed only once. The director Rob Bowman and producer Chris Carter would have a lot of film footage. They could choose the right moments from these film segments when they put the final movie together. When the director yelled "action," the explosives were set off. The drums of propane were ignited, or lit up. The entire facade blew up, with glass and other building materials flying into the air. At the same time that the building exploded, desks were thrown out of upper story windows. Cars parked around the building were made to jump up into the air by hydraulic jacks—machines that use liquid under a lot of pressure to move heavy things. The cars looked as if they had been hit by the force of the blast.

The car carrying Mulder and Scully was also lifted into the air by hydraulics. The car then swerved and crashed, sending bits of broken window glass flying into their faces. To protect the actors (stunt doubles, not David Duchovny and Gillian Anderson), pieces of rubber that looked like glass were shot from small cannons inside the car, toward their faces. Even the rubber pieces could have hurt the actors. So a clear piece of plastic was put in front of them, to shield them. Because the plastic was clear, it cannot be seen in the shot. It looks as if the "glass" is hitting the actors.

Paul Lombardi's crew were also responsible for blowing up cars.

Many times, the special effects crew has to create weather for movies. If a scene calls for rain, for example, it is the effects crew's job to create rain. If the movie is being filmed on a sunny day, or on a stage, the crew pumps in water through large hoses with nozzle sprays. Other times, a scene may call for wind when there is none. The effects crew will bring in giant fans to make a scene look windy.

Hollywood Special Effects was faced with just that kind of problem in *The X-Files* for the scene in which Mulder and Scully are chased through a cornfield in

Night shooting in a cornfield in Bakersfield included low-flying helicopters.

Texas by helicopters. The helicopters kick up dust and blow the cornstalks as they fly low to the field. It would have been too dangerous to have the helicopters really fly that low to the actors and the cornfield. So the dust and wind from the helicopters had to be created through special effects.

Four huge fans were set up around a small cornfield that was planted in a canyon in Southern California. When the director called "action," the fans were turned on. They blew the stalks of corn as Mulder and Scully ran through the field. To create flying dust, the special effects technicians had smoke generators at the location, too. The smoke generators pumped smoke out onto the field. They made it look like dust was swirling all around the two actors.

"Smoke isn't the most glamorous thing we do in special effects," Paul Lombardi commented, "but it is always one of the most difficult things."

For a later scene in the movie, the special effects team set fire to the cornfield. This was not as simple as just lighting a match to the stalks of corn. The corn was so green and wet it would not burn that easily. The effects crew had to bring in bales of dry hay which would burn well. They scattered the hay on the ground, between corn stalks. They also pumped in alcohol—a liquid that burns very easily—to soak the hay and corn and set them on fire.

In the middle of the cornfield, Mulder and Scully find two huge white domes, glowing eerily in the Texas night.

Bee dome interiors were filmed on stage at Fox, where bee wrangler
Dr. Norman Gary and his crew released 300,000 bees over
the course of three days of filming. Crew members shielded
themselves with special protective gear.

When they go inside the domes to investigate, the two
agents are chased by swarms of bees. To shoot the bee
scene, one of the domes was set up on a stage at Twentieth Century Fox. Bee expert Dr. Norman Gary released a
total of three hundred thousand real live bees inside the
dome over two days of filming.

Actors David Duchovny and Gillian Anderson and
most of the film crew were covered with a bug repellent.
This was to keep them from being stung. For each shot,
Dr. Gary released fifteen thousand bees from screened
cages into the stage. He did this by gathering them up
with a little scooper and tossing them into the air. (This

did not hurt the bees.) Dr. Gary could control the direction the bees flew by releasing a special pheromone. This is a kind of odor that the bees really liked and would follow. At the end of each "take," the bees were blown off the actors with big fans. Dead bees were glued onto the actors' clothes by the wardrobe department. This made it look as if Mulder and Scully were even more covered with the insects.

Only one bee was needed for a close-up shot of Scully being questioned by the FBI's office of professional review. A single bee travels along the collar of her jacket as Scully answers questions about her investigation in Texas with Mulder. Dr. Gary trained the bee to perform the stunt by leaving a trail of pheromone along Scully's

Producer Dan Sackheim and David Duchovny in the interior bee dome.

collar. The bee/actor not only performed the action perfectly once, but over and over again as the day of filming wore on!

As incredible as it may seem, none of the actors was stung by a bee through all the days of bee filming. "People are irrationally afraid of bees," Dr. Gary said. "It's funny. The same people who would work with a tiger and not think anything about it, get very upset at the thought of working with bees."

6
MODELS AND MAGIC

(VISUAL EFFECTS)

The live-action filming of *The X-Files* finished up in October 1997. But the movie was not yet completed. In the months to come, visual effects supervisor Mat Beck and his crew filmed models. They also created computer generated (CG) effects for some of the movie's most exciting scenes.

Mat Beck knew *The X-Files* inside and out. He had been the visual effects producer on the show for three years. He left to supervise the effects on the movie *Volcano*. Later, he worked on *Titanic*, creating some of that movie's iceberg shots.

For the scene in which a bomb goes off in the federal building, the production created an explosion in the real UNOCAL building in downtown Los Angeles. But a big part of the explosion still had to be finished with a building model. "In the movie," said visual effects producer Kurt Williams, "the whole building was supposed to be destroyed. But we couldn't destroy the entire UNOCAL building. So we just set off the explosion in the lower two levels of the real building, and used a model to show the rest of the building blowing up."

The building model was twenty-three feet tall. It was built by a model company called Hunter/Gratzner Industries. The model was made out of aluminum framing, with clear Plexiglas, or plastic, windows. The rooms that would be seen through those windows had to look real. So the model crew put in miniature desks, lamps, calendars, and other office furniture. Ian O'Connor is an expert in miniature pyrotechnics—or the science of setting off explosives. He rigged the building model with explosives to create billowing clouds of smoke. Several upper floors of the model were also rigged with release mechanisms. These let the crew collapse floors on cue, dumping debris and fake glass. After some cleanup, the floors could be set up again and the shot done another time.

The model was set up in the parking lot of the Hughes Aircraft facility. This was once a place where planes were built. Now it is a closed area that is often used for film production. Blue screen was set up on all sides of the model. Blue screen is like movie screen material that has been colored blue. The blue screen allowed the visual effects team to combine the model photography with the live-action that had been filmed in downtown Los Angeles. A shot that combines photography filmed at different times and at different locations is called a composite. It is similar to the effect you would get if you took a picture of your dog's head, for example, covering his body in blue screen. Then you could take a picture of your body, with your head covered in blue screen. If you lined up the two images just right, and had them printed together in a composite, you could make it look as if your dog's head was on your body.

For the building explosion, the visual effects crew had to line up the model so that it could be matched up with the real building. They could create a composite shot that looked as if the real UNOCAL building blew up and collapsed.

The visual effects team also built a miniature glacier for the scene at the end of the movie. This is the scene in which the spaceship rises from below the Antarctic ice. The model was hardly "miniature," however. It was sixty feet long and twenty feet wide. Set up on three large tabletops, the glacier model looked like a blanket of ice and snow. Regular table salt was laid out over the three tabletops to create fake snow.

The model was rigged so that large sections of the tabletop platform could be pulled out. This made the "snow" on top collapse. This rigging was needed for shots of Mulder and Scully running as the glacier caved in because of the spaceship rising from below. David Duchovny and Gillian Anderson, or their stunt doubles, were filmed in front of a green screen. (Green screen is similar to blue screen, but it is used when the actors are wearing blue clothing. In this scene, Mulder's costume

79

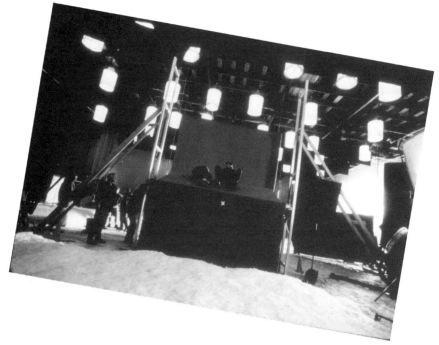

A special rig was devised to show Mulder and Scully
rising on a section of the spaceship.

was dark blue.) The green screen made it possible to take
just their images from the footage. It could then be composited into the footage of the miniature glacier.

One scene required a model spaceship. The spaceship
was seen rising from the ice and taking off into the sky as
Mulder and Scully watch. Two spaceship models were
actually built. One was a six-foot-in-diameter model of
the entire ship. This is the one that was seen in the sky.

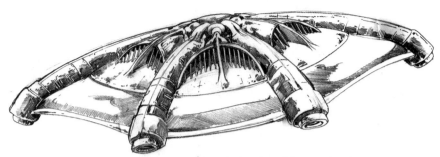

An early drawing of the exterior of the alien ship.

The second was a larger-scaled, twelve-foot section. This one was used just for shots of the spaceship rising up behind Mulder and Scully. The ship models were made out of plastics. The surfaces were made of scratched metals to look like details on the ship. Small lights were put inside to create an inner glow.

Both of the models were filmed separately, through a process called "motion control." Motion control means that the camera filming the ship is connected to a computer. The camera moves can be programmed into the computer and repeated exactly over and over again. This was necessary, since the ship models had to be filmed not just once, but several times. Each time is called a "pass." One pass was needed to film the model looking just right—called the "beauty pass." Another pass was done with the ship blacked out, and only the lights on the ship filmed—called the "light pass." Yet another pass was shot to provide a matte of the saucer. This "matte pass" could then be composited into the live-action or model photography. This created a ship-shaped "hole" that the beauty and light passes could be placed into.

The X-Files movie not only used models for visual effects shots. It also had several scenes with computer generated—CG—effects. CG is the technology that was used to create the dinosaurs for *Jurassic Park* and the bugs in *Starship Troopers*. If you have computer games at home, then you have already seen computer graphics. CG effects in the movies are just very advanced computer graphics.

One effect that was done with CG was the black, alien oil that travels up the primitive man's body at the beginning of the movie. The same substance is later seen moving into Stevie's shoe, then crawling and wriggling beneath his skin like worms. The visual effects team called both scenes the "worms sequences" since the blood looked and acted like worms.

How do you make liquid pool and wriggle? How do you make it move up a body? These were the problems the visual effects crew faced. They decided that the best way to solve them was to create the worms through CG. Then they composited those images with shots of the primitive and Stevie. First, the computer artists built a worm model in the computer. This three-dimensional—3D—model looked like a wire-frame object—almost as if it were made out of chicken wire. That created the basic shape. Then shaders were applied to the wire-frame model. These made it look black and shiny, like oil. Once one model was built, it could be copied to make as many worms as the visual effects team needed for each shot.

For the first worms scene, they also had to build a CG model of the primitive. That model was lined up with the real actor in each shot. With the CG version of the actor lined up on the computer screen, the computer team animated the CG worms to move up the primitive's body. When the CG elements had been composited with the live-action elements, the computer shots were made back into film. The film now showed the primitive reacting to black worms moving up his body, instead of reacting to things he could not see.

The Stevie/worms scene was a little more difficult. The black worms had to travel beneath his skin, rather than on top of it. In that case, the CG worms were animated—made to move—into a CG version of his shoe. A CG arm was modeled and "texture mapped" with the image of Stevie's real arm. This CG arm was used for shots of the worms moving beneath the skin of his arm. Texture mapping is a way of taking something from the filmed images—such as the skin of an arm—and wrapping it around a CG model on the computer. Planets in outer-space movies are often created this way. Artists take a sample of a photograph of Mars, for example, then wrap the colors and texture of that photograph around a CG, wire-frame globe. The same thing was done for Stevie's arm. The texture mapping made it *look* like his real arm. Since it was actually a CG arm, the digital artists could stretch it and warp it and make it wriggle as if the worms were crawling underneath.

More CG effects were needed for the scenes inside the spaceship. In the story, the spaceship is supposed to be huge—twelve hundred feet across, which is the size of four football fields lined up from end to end! It was impossible for the movie crew to build a spaceship that big. It would have cost millions and millions of dollars, and there was no stage big enough to build it on. For shots of the outside of the ship, they were able to build a smaller model and film that. When it was added to the live-action footage, it looked as if it was the right size. A model also could have been built for the *inside* of the spaceship to create the illusion of a huge space. The problem with doing that was that in almost every shot, Mulder was walking around the space. Just picture Mulder walking around miniature spaceship corridors. David Duchovny would look like a giant!

Another possible solution would have been to film a model of the inside of the spaceship. Then Duchovny could be filmed separately, against green screen or blue screen. Finally his image could have been shrunk down and composited into the film of the model spaceship. That kind of thing has been done a lot in the movies. Usually, it is done for scenes where there are only one or two shots of the person inside the model. It is difficult to composite the green screen or blue screen actor into film of the model. It is hard to get it matched up just right in closeups and to make it look as if his feet are really touching the floor of the model. It is also difficult to match the lighting exactly, so that the light hitting the model matches the light hitting the actor. Watch old science-fiction movies closely. You will notice that the lighting on the giant spider, for example, doesn't match the lighting on the street he is walking down at all! That's because the spider was shot at a different time and in a different place than the street.

The movie climax takes place within the interior of a spaceship, settled beneath the ice in Antarctica.

The best solution was to build as much of the inside of the spaceship on stage as was possible. Those were the areas that Mulder would be seen walking on. In the background, the real set would be made to look much bigger with CG set extensions. Blue or green screens were hung all around the top of the real spaceship interior set. They were hung from pipes that were attached to the ceiling of the stage. This gave the visual effects artists a blue or green matte area into which they could add CG sets.

Those sets started as CG models. They were painted and textured to match the real set. Live-action footage from the real set—footage with David Duchovny in the hallways, for example—was scanned into the computer. The CG spaceship interior models were then added to the matte areas. The new composite shots were scanned back out to film.

Even though the movie finished shooting early in October, the visual effects team worked up until the following May. They continued shooting models and creating CG shots. Little by little, those effects shots were added to the movie. In May, the producers finally had a completed movie with spaceships, a huge spaceship interior, black worms, glaciers caving in, and exploding buildings!

All together, *The X-Files* movie required two and a half months of preparation and five months of filming. After it was all down on film it took another six months to complete the visual effects shots and edit the movie. Finally music and sound effects were added. The movie was completed at last. At the end of May 1998, thousands of copies of the movie were made. They went out to theaters all over the country for a June 1998 release.